DID HIP HOP
KILL
Jesus?

Did Hip-Hop Kill Jesus?

©Copyright 2012-Dr. Tyree Williams.

All rights reserved. No part of this book may be reproduced or transmitted in any form or by any means, electronic, or mechanical, including photocopying and recording, or by any information storage and retrieval system, without permission in writing from the publisher.

All Scripture quotations, unless otherwise identified, are taken from the HOLY BIBLE, NEW INTERNATIONAL VERSION®, (NIV) ®Copyright © 1973, 1978, 1984 International Bible Society. Used by permission of Zondervan Publishing House. All rights reserved. Scripture quotations marked (KJV) are take from the King James Version. Used by permission of NavPress Publishing Group. All rights reserved. Please note that MarkOne publishing style capitalizes certain pronouns in Scripture that refer to the Father, Son, and Holy Spirit, and may differ from some publishers' styles.

ISBN 978-0-9857849-3-5

Library of Congress Cataloging –in-Publication Data:

An application to register this book for Cataloging has been submitted to the Library of Congress. Printed in the USA and Canada.

Cover, book, and interior design by KDR Consulting, LLC ®

Published By MarkOne Publishing
3645 Marketplace Blvd, Suite 130-370
Atlanta, Georgia 30344
A subsidiary of KDR Consulting, LLC

Acknowledgements

A Note from Sis. Diann Williams:

I could not have accomplished any of this without the help of my Lord and Savior Jesus Christ and the greatest support group in the world: Dad, Mom, Mr. Oliver Monroe, Sr., and Mrs. Roy Monroe (the latter two of which celebrate their 70th wedding anniversary on December 25, 2012). In addition, I would like to acknowledge my 10 remaining siblings and the entire Monroe family. I also recognize the special help I've received from Marilyn Monroe-Young and my church family, thank you. I love you and thank you all for loving me. Special recognition to Dr. Angela Washington at United Theological Seminary, my friend Gwendolyn Carter, and the KDR Consulting, LLC family for their awesome help and resources provided to me during the course of bringing forth Pastor Williams' vision. Well Done. To God Be The Glory.

Rev. Dr. Tyree Williams
August 31, 1955 – October 6, 2011

Contents

Introduction 1

CHAPTER ONE From Generation to Generation 5

CHAPTER TWO Drinking From the Fountain of Change. 19

CHAPTER THREE From E. F. Hutton to Mark Zukerburg 31

CHAPTER FOUR The Church Of Stipulations Minus God in Christ 43

CHAPTER FIVE We Worship Better Together. 55

CHAPTER SIX Out of the Mouths of Babes 65

CHAPTER SEVEN The Do Something Experience 77

CHAPTER EIGHT Plenty Good Room 87

References 95

Introduction

"Precious Lord, Take My Hand," has been, for generations one of the most noted and sacred songs of the church. Many have considered this song the corner stone of gospel music. This spiritual masterpiece has been sung at funerals, during the high point of Sunday morning services, and even as vows are read in wedding ceremonies. The writer of this powerful musical gem, Thomas A. Dorsey, has been heralded as the man who created the genre we now know as black gospel music. Dorsey stated that he began to develop this sacred style based on the syncopated notes and structure of blues.

He customized and developed a new sound by substituting the themes of defiance, in the face of utter despair in secular blues, with the good news of God's love, His hope, and faith. As I read and researched Mr. Dorsey's biography, I noted that he was a product of the church, was the son of a preacher, and grew up in the south. Yet, after dropping out of school at age 11, he headed north for Chicago. Thomas began to develop into a prominent pianist in the city's premier secular nightclubs and blues joints.

Did Hip Hop Kill Jesus?

After a series of nervous breakdowns that affected his health and musical stability, Mr. Dorsey made the decision to devote his life, gifts, and energies towards doing the Lord's work. This great hymn of the church was birthed out of immense tragedy. Thomas' wife and son both died during childbirth, throwing his life into a tailspin. In an effort to deal with his grief, Mr. Dorsey found solace in turning to his piano. "Take My Hand, Precious Lord," was born.

I found it quite interesting that through all of this, gospel music was almost aborted due to the fact that the church rejected his calling simply because of the sound and newness he delivered. Dorsey has been quoted as saying, "I've been thrown out of some of the best churches in America." In his attempt to do what he was called to do and birth a revolution in the church, he returned to the secular music business full-time. He met an immense amount of disdain and rejection from pastors and churches because they considered his "gospel" the "devil's music."

Can you imagine the 21st century and church without gospel music? So many people have been helped, so many dark days have been made light, and so many burdens have been lifted because of this music. A young man was almost about to abort his calling because older, more traditional mindsets said that this did not fit their definition of religion and Christianity.

There are innumerable Thomas Dorseys in the streets, homes, communities, and churches of inner city urban

Introduction

America, yet, a generation of traditionalist, passive dream killers, and aggressive anti-change agents, are unable to allow the products of Generation X to have a voice or express their thoughts. Is this a proponent of faith or a product of fear?

Dr. Tyree Williams, a theologian and successful pastor of a historic and predominantly traditional church in inner city Cleveland, Ohio has mastered and customized the art of developing cohesive relationships, atmospheres, and ministry that span four generations. This literary gem provides the tools, insight, and spiritual structure to attract and retain the youth and young adults in your church, neighborhood, and community. Congruently, this book will assist in cultivating your adults and seasoned membership in the support, encouragement, and understanding of their junior counterparts.

I challenge you to use this book as a guide for church growth, community development, and even succession planning for the life and longevity of any ministry, regardless of size, denomination, culture, or worship style. A Thomas Dorsey-styled revolution could very well be in our midst. Will your ministry, or you as a member, be an incubator for growth or a chamber for its demise?

Let's journey deeper as we grow in understanding.

CHAPTER ONE

From Generation to Generation

Is it truly possible for the message and spirit of Jesus to live if He is only relevant and embraced by a limited generation?

Is Christianity truly Christianity if I only see Christ from my perspective and eliminate the views of others because of age or generation?

If Jesus' message expires in relevance after those born in 1984, is it truly the gospel?

The movement or religion of hip-hop, much like Christianity, was shunned and cast away as an irrelevant fad by its early opposition. Yet, its founders and forefathers believed that this platform of expression would be the next wave of musical and cultural formalism. With the usage of albums, sampling of legendary artists' songs and words, and the creation of a sound that had never been expressed, hip-hop was born.

Did Hip Hop Kill Jesus?

Despite the skeptics and naysayers, this cultural religion has transformed into the business, lifestyle, music, and communication of everyday living. After almost five decades of this creation, there is now a generation that lives, breathes, and operates under the premise of this urban concept. With this being the mechanism by which everything from real estate to religion is distributed and communicated, how can the church turn their backs on a generation that moves in a similar vein and footprint?

The questions that must be considered are:

> Will churches allow hip-hop to do to Jesus what Roman crucifixion was unable to do?

> Will it kill Him?

I must make a confession. I love music!

Make no mistake about it; this is one form of communication that requires no translation. Regardless of your native language, ethnic background, or age, everyone understands the message of music. It has been said that music is the true charmer of the soul. Yet, it amazes me how often we allow this same music to divide us spiritually. This passionate, poetic portal has been the platform by which so many generations express, challenge, and define the occurrences of their time.

Despite this understanding, in many traditional churches, we have allowed the music of this age to force us into a state of trouble. What kind of trouble? The kind that has often handicapped our ministries, isolated potential believers, and minimized the spiritual impact in our society.

Even more insidious is the fact that many churches are in trouble and have decided that they either don't recognize it or don't care. Where is this trouble stemming from? It stems from the elimination of an entire generation of people that are not welcome as a part of the organization called church. The eliminated generation is today's youth.

Please understand that as a man in my fifties, I am not attempting to relive my youth. I often times embody the same likes, dislikes, aches and pains of a middle-aged man, yet my heart has always been in tune with young people. Perhaps my fondness for the youth stemmed from the fact that I entered into ministry at the tender age of twenty.

Realize that when a whole generation of people are absent from an organization whose principles and beliefs rest upon embracing all generations, the organization is not living up to its intended mission. The church, therefore, is not merely an organization, but a living organism. It is a picture and image of the body of Jesus Christ in our world. When this organism allows the platform of music to be a virus instead of an antidote, disease will soon set in.

The great Christian pastor, author, and consultant, Gary L. McIntosh, in his book *One Church Four Generations* states:

> *"As I have traveled, consulting with churches and leading church growth seminars during the past eighteen years, I have noticed that most churches target one generation*

exclusively-Builder or Boomers or Busters or Bridgers-while often ignoring the others. More importantly, in many mainline traditional urban churches in America, the youth are the group that is most often being ignored."

Recognize that this is not *always* done intentionally (although it is often done); indeed, some traditional churches have made valiant efforts towards reaching the youth and young adults. Nevertheless, these attempts lack substance because many churches usually have not been willing to take the "real steps" necessary to continually attract the youth.

I understand that the individuals who attend our churches and cathedrals are not bad people, contrarily; most of them are Godly people who simply refuse to recognize that their way of "doing" church is not the only way.

The computer is an amazing invention; nevertheless, I am unable and unrealistic if I attempt to use my 1987 IBM floppy disk computer to meet technological needs today. Yes, it is a PC, but by 21st century standards, it is simply not viable. We no longer use floppy disks to save data and the computers of that timeframe are not Internet or Wi-Fi compatible.

One of the main reasons that this hip-hop generation is being missed in our spiritual culture and society is because many streamlined, traditional churches embrace policies, traditions, and methods of worship that do not relevantly support the current urban culture and plight. It is virtually impossible to embrace and welcome an individual without clearly acknowledging and respecting what they view as relevant. Please understand, there is nothing wrong with the traditional and older ways in which ministry is carried out by our more seasoned parishioners, yet these modes of worship are foreign to this new and young generation.

Plethoras of scholars have arrived at a conclusion about the state of traditional churches. Alan Nelson and Gene Appel state in their book, *How to Change Your Church (Without Killing It)*:

> *"We do not believe there is a need to compromise on the basic tenants of the Bible or Christianity in order to bear fruit. At the same time, we know that many traditional congregations are designed to be productive in social settings reflective of the fifties through seventies-not the twenty-first century- in America."*

This concept is not limited to the smaller ministry congregations; even your larger churches with abundant weekly participation seem to be only maintaining, if they overlook the significant youth population. Eventually, they too will find their ministries in impending trouble. This is because older members will eventually die and without youth succession, these members will not be replaced.

Maintenance cannot be the goal of the church. Reproduction and continual revolution must be a part of the plan. If any organism or organization does not reproduce or grow, it will eventually die. In contrast to popular belief, churches, unlike businesses, do not plateau. Thom S. Rainer, the author of the book, *Break Out Churches,* states that:

> *"There is no such thing as a plateaued church. A church is either growing or declining. In my research of thousands of churches, I have never seen a church maintain identical statistics for more than two consecutive years."*

How beautiful would the gift of life be if only one or two age ranges lived and then died? If new life was not birthed into our world, if a different thought process was never embraced, or if progress was halted at your job once you retired, would the value and experience of life remain the same? There are clear lessons to be learned from the youth we shun about fostering true Christianity. Listening ears and clearer minds must prevail in this endeavor.

Developing a Mindset of Change

> *"Some churches, fearing worldly infection, retreat into isolation from today's culture. While most do not retreat as far back as the Amish have, many churches seem to think that the 1950s was the golden age, and they are determined to preserve that era in their church. What I admire about the Amish is at least they are honest about it. They freely admit that they have chosen to preserve the*

> *lifestyle of the 1800s. In contrast, churches that try to perpetuate the culture of the 1950s usually deny their intent or they try to prove with proof-texts that they are doing it the way it was done in New Testament times."*

This quote from Rick Warren's monumental book, *The Purpose Driven Church*, clarifies the conundrum of the modern day church in a post-modern society. With the imminent rise of post-modernism, a lack of clarity has fostered the challenges and conflicts with the unchanging truth in Christian society. The Christian concept stands on the belief that absolute truth is found only in the Bible. The moral teachings, assertions about one true God, the Lordship of Christ, and His substitutionary death are all absolutes in the Christian faith. With changing perceptions of truth in this current age, foundational concepts must be established and effectively taught.

Post-modernism challenges these absolutes and sees truth as relative. This concept embraces a form of 'whatever works for you' gospel. For this hip-hop saturated generation of young people, who for the most part have not been previously exposed to Christian principles, scripture, and lifestyle, post-modernism can be quite attractive. Honestly, even for many of those who have been exposed to Christian principles, scripture, and lifestyle, post-modernism can be a concept that is flirted with in a passive manner.

Although many young people may not be aware of

the phrase 'post-modernism,' they are bombarded with its prevailing influence daily. We must understand that the conflicting paradox of this trend hinges on the fact that most generations prior to post-modernism (roughly the periods before the sixties) did not question and challenge Christian absolutes as much as they do today. It many cases, it was never questioned at all.

Once, the most astute and scholarly individual in American urban communities was the pastor or clergyman. I have found that, in any given congregation and community, a large percentage of the young adult population has earned some form of post-secondary educational success. With continual advancement in technology, the advent of the World Wide Web and the ability for millions to access information 24-hours-a-day, every aspect of life is constantly and aggressively questioned on all ends.

Of course, there are many who have chosen not to become Christians at all. As a pastor of a growing congregation in inner city America, it has become clear to me that many non-believers have decided not to accept the truths of Christianity or were drawn to other teachings that they believed to be absolute truths, but rarely was their decision because there was no absolute truth. This is a major challenge that faces young people in regards to church. We will delve into these concerns in detail as we progress in the book.

The church as a whole has barely changed in the last 50 years. During a period in which the culture of church remained the same, yet the mindset of people have evolved so drastically, the old church model often lacks the ability to effectively evangelize and draw new believers to Christ for more than a brief season. With such a massive generation gap between the old church and the present, the bridge of change must be built and embraced for Christ and His church to survive.

It is often hard to embrace that which we do not understand, particularly when it looks and sounds foreign. Hip-hop culture encompasses so much more than sagging jeans, tattoos, and bass-laden music. It is truly a religion. This culture has stood the test of time. Its fans span not only youth, but older people as well. We see it in every avenue of life, yet the only platform of our culture that forcibly resists its influence is the church.

It is worthy to note that so many moves of the Christian church were met with great resistance and disdain in their early onset. Therefore, it seems somewhat frivolous and hypocritical to declare an all-out disregard and deaf ear for those who desire to worship in a manner that mirrors their place of expression and understanding. Is this not what Christianity and Christ are all about? Where does the conversion and the conflict start? Will it ever end?

Unfortunately, human nature does not change. The pure traditionalist will, by nature, want to reject new things. This type of rejection is not a new concept; it has been this way throughout the annals of time. This is why education is so important. Dan Southerland, in his book, *Transitioning*, highlights this concept:

> *"For example, hymns are a tradition in many of our churches today. Yet, when hymns were first written, they were rejected by many because they consisted of spiritual words put to the common tunes of the day. (Both Calvin and Luther hired secular songwriters to take the popular bar tunes of the day and put their lyrics to them). When those hymns were later collected and put into a book of songs called a hymnal, they were again rejected by many who claimed that you could not worship God from the heart if you were singing from a book (I guess they were not aware that Psalms is a collection of the songs of the Hebrews-which makes it one of the first hymnals)."*

By no means is this a diatribe against the church or the older parishioners and seasoned saints; contrarily, this is a manifesto of seemingly unclear realities sacrificing a generation of potential believers for the sake of traditionalism. The inability to embrace a faith that is free to all in turn creates a new mission of 21st century crucifixion; due to a marriage between the church and past generations.

Conflict in Christianity

No matter how much we consider and theorize change,

friction will arise. The hope and desire is to keep this friction to a minimum, thereby achieving the predominant goal: the continual life and effectiveness of the church. Change, even in a positive state, can be traumatic for anyone, especially when an individual or group of individuals has been doing one thing for a long period, as have church traditionalists. Hence, I feel it necessary to have a section that spotlights the viewpoints of various conflict concepts and research regarding conflict in the church holistically.

With the focus being placed clearly on hip-hop, not as a genre, but a culture, I must highlight the observation of conflict in the African-American church:

> *"...while the African-American church is as likely as any other to have conflicts arising from the incompatible actions and activities of persons and groups, we can at least take hope that there are relatively few differences in the area of belief. While some churches may have conflicts over dogma, African-American churches are more likely to experience conflicts relative to issues of power, position, and money-issues that fall into the second and third categories of the above definition."*

According to the excerpt from author Dr. Lora-Ellen McKinney's book, *Getting to Amen*, there is a clear conflict in the African-American church on major issues of change. They must be addressed so that Jesus is not killed afresh by the conflicting views of traditional Christianity. Although this book only deals with conflict in regards to changing traditional churches and not the subject of change in general, its point is relevant because it is important to successfully implement change that anticipates conflict and attempts to avoid it beforehand.

It has been noted that conflict can be seen as a variable in the churches equation to solve for true intimacy. Any church that can find the ability to manage their passion-based conflicts and the litany of other issues that occur will be well equipped to engage ministry effectively and successfully on a maximum level. When this is embraced and understood, church effectiveness will initiate an embrace of the younger generation and encourage a sustained incentive for harmony between both groups.

The reason that young people no longer attend church as they once did is not the direct fault of the church. One can clearly place the majority of churches in one of two categories:

- ❖ **Traditionalist/Resistor**
- ❖ **Innovator/Embracer**

These categories are self-explanatory in nature. The context from which I pen this book is Traditionalist/Resistor. The platform of conflict manifests from the traditional, older church generation, and because this sect has been 'doing church' their way for so long, they have a natural tendency to resist change, thereby creating conflict on some level.

The overarching goal of this book is to present a process whereby the church as a whole can move into a realm of being an Innovator/Embracer church, thereby meshing the sound and strong qualities of traditionalism with the innovative, energetic, and fresh insights of the youthful, hip-hop generation.

I remember growing up with an old, rotary telephone in my mother's home. It sat on a small table in her living room and required me to dial only seven numbers to reach the person I was attempting to contact. Rarely, if ever, did I find myself writing down a number, unless it was an important one. When I did write, I placed it in a little black book or a rolodex. As technology advanced, the telephones transformed from a rotary dial to the touchtone format. No longer was I required to turn the dial; I was now able to press the buttons on the phone to contact a desired caller.

Many older individuals were not major fans of this development; because they had grown accustomed to the convenience of the rotary phone. So many phone communication progressions have been experienced since its inception: the pager, the portable phone, the Smart phone. The phone has changed so much since Alexander Graham Bell created it years ago. Yet, resistance to its advancements would only yield many unable to communicate on a daily basis. If not embraced, several people would soon find themselves in a silo or totally incapacitated.

This book's goal is not to change the principles and

truths of Christianity, but simply to open the dialogue and channels of communication in the traditional church. The hip-hop generation is merely the Smartphone of Christianity: retaining a "rotary phone traditionalist approach" will either totally incapacitate Jesus Christ or halt the ability for church to communicate effectively to the world.

The only question that must be answered in these next few chapters is, "Can you hear me now?"

CHAPTER TWO

Drinking From the Fountain of Change

I recall watching an episode on one of my favorite channels, Animal Planet, as they highlighted a documentary of a species of dinosaur known as the Plateosaurus. This particular dinosaur is the best studied of any early dinosaurs by scientist. In its adult form, it probably weighed close to a ton and easily reached a height of 15 feet when standing on its rear legs.

Because of their long necks, they always fed on high vegetation, such as leaves and ferns. Due to their lightly built skulls, it was suggested that these dinosaurs fed on soft plants, thereby, setting the example for later species of Mesozoic animals and the giraffes we know of today. These dinosaurs the part of Europe that now includes Germany, France, and Switzerland. They dominated this region for several years.

The most interesting aspect of this show came when the narrator explained that this particular dinosaur became extinct due to starvation. I was shocked by this statement. The narrator went on to explain that due to the Plateosaurus' comfort level and habit of feeding on extremely high vegetation, eventually, all of the high vegetation was consumed and eliminated. When this occurred, the dinosaurs ceased to eat. The researcher states that if only the animal would have bent their necks slightly to partake of the lower level vegetation, instead of always seeking the high hanging leaves, their life span would have been much longer.

I find it so intriguing that our previous generations of "Plateosuarus Christians" have been equipped with the tools to bless God, the world, and generations to come. We have, for long periods, watched and received God's blessings through turbulent and challenging times, social issues, and financial inconsistency. We have experienced days that look impossible, yet somehow, the Lord brought us through. The church has been able to eat from the "high vegetation" due to extreme growth, high visibility, and relative acceptance in the global society.

Along the way, the world, our visibility, and society began to change. Nonetheless, we decided to stay the same. Ideologies that we once stood strong on began to waiver and new generations were excluded instead of embraced by our "high vegetation" mindset. We woke in the 21st century on the verge of extinction. We are not here because of the lack of nutrients and vegetation. We are here now and will teeter on the verge of extinction due to our inability to bend or change. This lack of willingness currently attributes to the smaller percentage of children and young adults that go to church in urban areas in comparison to rural areas.

It seems that many of our traditional churches have been overtaken with a concern for the maintenance of the status quo, rather than actually reaching out to those who are "unchurched" and desirous of a better life. Unfortunately, the hip-hop generation suffers because of this mindset and focus. I have found that the churches that consistently minister to the "unchurched" are the ones that find themselves experiencing regular growth. The recognition must be centered on the concept that the most conducive form of ministry is outreach, not "inreach."

The successful churches of the 21st century have learned how to bend. They recognize that you must involve real people to grow real ministry. Many of the mainstream churches in the United States are saturated with older members. Therefore, the style, the tone, and the message is controlled and naturally geared towards them. The traditional ways of yesteryear, the ways that they were nurtured on, attract and appeal only them. In an effort to attract a younger demographic, the result will always be failure when using this as a road map for evangelism.

Recognize that churches have a right to their preference, however, in the church, believers are called to be concerned about the desires of the entire body, not simply their own. The church, in its purest state, is in the business of reaching out to those who are different; in this context, the hip-hop generation fits this description. Mainline older churches must start drinking from the fountain of change to remain relevant, effective, and alive.

> *The Church in America is in desperate need of a new model for the local church. We currently develop churches based on a model of ministry that was developed several hundred years ago, rejecting the fact that the society for which that model was designed no longer exists. The constant cry of the Unchurched-"the church is irrelevant to the way I live"-cannot be addressed until the model itself is renewed to acknowledge that the times have changed. Our approach to meeting people's needs with the unchanging truths of the gospel... (Barna, 1997).*

This quote, from George Barna's book, *User Friendly Churches*, lays a clear blueprint for the type of change that must be oriented into the fabric of today's ministry goals. With the values of people so drastically and rapidly changing, the concept of loyalty in the long-term is seemingly becoming a curse word.

We are currently in a time where there are, and may never be again, jobs that people sustain for 30 and 40 years. Businesses have diminished their desire or request for this level of loyalty. People no longer purchase homes with the vision of being in that same home for the rest of their lives. With all these things being different, how can church stay the same?

Much like the dinosaur, the church has eaten up the high hanging leaves and foliage, yet, there is a plethora of vegetation "beneath them." We must first be willing to bend in new ways, to be flexible for our mission. The important thing is that some progress must be made in the direction of change to develop and embrace this generation in the things of God. This must be initiated at the local church level, before it can be embraced as a national phenomenon.

If the church is to continue being successful by bringing the youth/young adult generation back into the fold, it will only occur when the church is fervent in trying to meet the needs of this mission field. There must be a concentrated interest and emphasis placed on the meeting the needs of the seeking hip-hop generation. You must address a few questions to make this concept effective:

> *What is it that young people actually need?*
>
> *Why are they shying away from your church?*
>
> *What would make young people more excited about your ministry?*
>
> *What could your church do to embrace much needed change?*

One of the aspects that are central to the existence of the church is the worship time of the church and the times of its collective gatherings. Of course, worship occurs most frequently during regular Sunday morning Worship Service. Yet, the concept of developing a true worship experience is more relevant biblically, and in this generation, than worship timeframes. One example of that is:

> *Every day they continued to meet together in the temple courts. They broke bread in their homes and ate together with glad and sincere hearts, Acts 2:46-47 (NIV)*

The reality is that Sunday service is the time that most seekers (non-believers who are interested in spiritual things) and pre-Christians get their initial impressions of the church, be it positive or negative. This is the main reason why the Apostle Paul was so concerned that the church at Corinth made use of its spiritual gifts in a proper and fitting way:

> *So it the whole church comes together and speaks in tongues, and inquirers or unbelievers come in, will they not say that you are out of your mind? But if an unbeliever or an inquirer comes in while everyone is prophesying, they are convicted of sin and are brought under judgment by all, as the secrets of their hearts are laid bare. So they will fall down and worship God, exclaiming "God is really among you!" I Corinthians 14:23-25 (NIV)*

This is not to simply highlight the spiritual of speaking in tongues, yet the message that is being conveyed is one that is extremely relevant to the concept of embracing this generation. You can get caught up and excited in the things of your traditional or spiritual upbringing that those in your age group can relate to, but does it bespeak Christ to a younger generation? They may not grasp this channel of communication, but the seeker, pre-Christian, or young adult will be drawn to the simple proclamation of Jesus Christ in your life and within their context of understanding. Now, true ministry will occur that is not limited to age, experience, or gift. It erases all lines of separation and viewpoint.

Paul understood that *how* they worshiped would affect a visitor's perception of the church. Although this particular passage is specific to the gift of speaking in tongues, the underlying principle is that the worship service must not be completely foreign to unbelievers who might attend. People could perceive this as a total turn off, not simply to your church, but to church as a whole.

While believers primarily attend the church worship experience, it must not be totally foreign to unbelievers, either. The challenge that must be overcome is the ability to incorporate everyone in the worship experience and alienate no one. When there are foreign concepts that are prevalent in the church, they must be rendered translatable, simplified, or combined with other corporate concepts. I have recognized that some traditional approaches to worship have become too 'foreign' for certain sects of the population.

The worship experience is when the church is at its largest in numbers and potentially at its greatest level of strength. This is why all ministries must focus primarily, yet not exclusively, on the worship experience as a tool for outreach.

We must understand that the church membership is more than just Sunday worship, yet Sunday worship is usually the door by which others enter into full church membership. If that which resides inside of the door is not attractive, or at least interesting, they will likely not enter or remain therein.

When we place a more clear focus on the worship styles of the urban African-American churches of today, the worship experience is comparable to that of the decades of the forties and fifties. The service is lively and spirited, yet it lacks the contemporary element. I find that this is the primary reason so many churches are predominantly made up of a significantly senior crowd. The balance structure is uneven because of the absence of the youth and young adult parishioner. The gap between infants and the forty plus crowd is problematic for the life of the church.

It is understood that the term "marketing" is looked down on in many traditional churches. Although this term engenders images from the business and corporate world, Christians are called to evangelize in the world and to proclaim the gospel throughout the world. Like it or not, this is the essence of what marketing really is. In marketing, this concept is simply called the target market, yet in the religious arena, it is considered a mission field. Clearly highlighting this as an area of focus is important.

George Barna states in his book, *Marketing the Church*:

> *I believe that as we begin to understand the basic element of marketing, we will find*

countless examples of marketing activity in the Bible. Many of the efforts of Jesus and His disciples represent lessons in marketing and ought to reduce our concern that marketing, as a way of approaching Christian ministry, is not biblically sound." (Barna, 1988).

Understanding the changing culture of the times provides churches and pastors with the ability of knowing what the community in which your church resides needs and how best to meet them. Once you are able to determine what people are desirous of and the opportunities that exist for developing a solution for the needs, you stand a great chance for fulfilling that need by developing an action plan that will find acceptance in the marketplace.

The worst thing that you can do as a church attempting to change is to start a revolution that has no focus or validity. You must have a strategy and a plan of action to effect a thorough change. Once the right tactics are known, then those new things are to be instituted, and the targeted group is to be invited. Usually, most people are invited by word-of-mouth, but other more formal ways of getting the message out can be used, as well.

Young people will most certainly tell other young people when something interesting is happening in their church. When you excite or engage the hip-hop generation, they instantly become your greatest marketing tool. You have to grab the young people on the level that they are on. Much like the sport of fishing, different fish eat different bait. You will not be able to catch all fish with the same lure.

Understanding their perspective gains trust and thereby gains a level of comfort to break down the barriers that currently stand. One of the first steps that must be taken to affect a more attractive appeal to the hip-hop generation begins by re-educating the traditionalists and older people who are already within your church. It will be difficult for an 80-year-old woman to be highly effective as a kindergarten teacher.

This is by no means a gender bias statement and it is not impossible. Yet, for the teacher to be successful, she must be able to play, crawl, and tumble on the floor with ease. It would also be beneficial if the teacher add an understanding of kid's programs, toys, and interest to keep them engaged. Without this connection, the age difference for the teacher and the children could be a major area of conflict.

With the re-educating of the traditional concept, the connecting points can be more clearly outlined and the blurred lines of traditionalism can be cleared up. This is beneficial because there are several misunderstandings, differences, and dislikes that

It must be discussed and shared in sermons, Sunday school, training classes, and other conversational mediums. They must see why a new way of doing church is completely in order if the next generation is to be reached. When the changes are talked about *before* they are implemented, it avoids the accusation that some might make regarding the fact that leadership just "sprung this change on us." It is important to garner the enthusiasm of the traditionalist to implement an effective and thorough change. In addition, from a more positive perspective, it gives the traditionalist an opportunity to get on board with the changes. It also provides the pastorate with the 'by in' from these traditionalist.

Understand that during this process of change, you will be able to spot the individuals who have the creativity to help bring about this change in a relevant way. You will also come into contact with those who are highly opinionated in regards to any direction that you endeavor to implement change. Next, you will find the people who will immediately get on board and a segment of the group that will get on board, but at a later date. Finally, be prepared for those who are set to resist change, no matter what you do or say.

The smallest group will be comprised of the individuals who have the creativity to help bring about the change. The highly opinionated generally make up a small percentage of the congregation and they will be your method of communication, whether positive or negative. Those who get on board immediately or later are in the 30 percentile of your congregation. As outlined, they will "get on board", yet, it is only a matter of when they will decide. The communications of the highly opinionated are the determining factors of this time-based decision.

Finally, the change resistant will never be on board. They make up about 15% of the congregation and they will be a part of the change, yet they will never agree or support its overall focus.

Did Hip Hop Kill Jesus?

Recognize that it is human nature to resist change, yet it is also a reality that change must and will occur. The need is great and the benefits of fulfilling the need are endless. The hip-hop generation must be embraced, involved, and understood, because they are conduits for the continual spreading of the gospel and proponents for the continual life of the church.

I recognized that while watching the documentary of the Plateosarus on Animal Planet that this dinosaur was once a powerful, dominant, and massive force on our planet. As they grew and matured, they developed multiple species of their own kind. They ate where and when they chose and were beneficial to society as a whole. There was only one problem…they refused to change when change was necessary.

It has been millions of years since they roamed the planet and their extinction could have been avoided or postponed with the simple decision to bend a little. There are some clear ails and ills found in this hip-hop generation; yet, there were some ails and ills in my generation, as well. Imagine the outcome if someone in the church refused to make a slight change to embrace my generation. Where would we be? Being a member of the baby boomer generation, I understand that every generation has its pros and cons; nevertheless, they deserve to be understood and embraced.

Learn to drink from this fountain…the water is sweet, refreshing, and plenteous enough that everyone can quench their thirst. Embrace the change, so that the change will spread the message of the Savior.

CHAPTER THREE

From E. F. Hutton to Mark Zukerburg

Since I was a kid, I have been an avid sports fan. Growing up in Cleveland, Ohio, football was always a way of life. The Browns are my favorite team, win, lose, or draw; that will never change. Interestingly, one of my fondest memories of watching football in the late seventies and early eighties comes not from the sport itself, but from a commercial that would appear religiously during every game.

These commercials would generally include two middle-aged men either jogging in a park or walking through an airport. One of the men would speak of some long-term investment concerns he had mentioned to his broker. Seeking a second opinion, he would ask the other fellow of his broker's opinion. With perfect confidence and timing, the retort would always be, "My broker is E. F. Hutton, and he says…" At that point, no matter where the conversation took place, everyone would come to a screeching halt and silence would overtake the locale.

The 30-second slot would end with an announcer stating that, "When E. F. Hutton talks, people listen." What a powerful statement! Edward Francis Hutton, along with his brother, developed one of the most respected and notable financial firms in the United States. In a time of international turmoil, high interest rates, and rising political instability, this firm and this name were an image of trust, confidence, and great service.

This firm and its commercial define a generation and a mindset. As a result of financial changes, court cases, and mergers, E. F. Hutton has ceased to be a firm for more than 20 years. They have recently opened their doors in a much smaller and intimate fashion, yet, nothing reflective of their previous success.

So much has changed since Hutton's closed its doors years ago. He is no longer the voice that people listen to. Instead, the voice that people of today listen to is not a financial guru and brokerage powerhouse; it's that of a young, computer programmer turned entrepreneur: Mark Zuckerburg. This youngster is the brainchild behind the worldwide phenomenon called Facebook, the social media tool that has made the world smaller and more intimate with the simple click of a button. It is important that churches recognize the "voice" of the day.

As a church, you must be able to effectively deliver the message of yesterday by using the clarion voice of today. However, if you are not sure of the most effective way to deliver the message, it will come across as totally unclear. So, let's begin to understand the voice of this generation.

Many of the aspects of the hip-hop generation hinge on the muddy concept of respect and independence. It is predicated on the notion of a generation that has received overwhelming criticism, yet minimum support for their inadequacies. The voice of this generation centers itself around convenience, acceptance, and uniqueness. The church must learn to highlight this generation's strengths and benefits, as opposed to pinpointing the weaknesses or deficiencies.

Churches in the previous decade centered and categorized sin and wrongdoing in a manner that simply focused on trusting God, reading the Bible, and living right. Yet, what does a ministry say to the young woman or young man who was molested by his father, abused repeatedly by a clergy person, or raised without a father or a mother? Is the simple fix continually going to be trust God, read the Bible, and live right? There must be a process in place to minister to the issues and concerns of this day and age that incorporates life application and problem resolution. Churches need to equip themselves to support and heal this generation.

In the 21st century ministry, we are totally unprepared to handle the current issues this generation faces. While attempting to redefine our churches, we must also realign our hearts to embrace a generation that is unchurched and unfamiliar with the protocols and culture of the traditional church. It cannot be totally attire-focused, yet it must be spiritually focused on the development and growth of a new soul to the Body of Christ.

A contemporary mindset must be designed and embraced. This mindset is one that considers and operates in the current age and time. The phenomenon of the 'contemporary church' is relatively new. The misnomer that this concept is isolated to the mega-church has been developed because traditional churches have shunned meeting the desperate needs the hip-hop generation has long and loudly cried out for. Contemporary churches, therefore, are meeting needs that are seemingly ignored in so many other places.

I have nothing but praise for what the contemporary church is doing through their vehicle of creative and customized worship. The contemporary church dares to be different and it embraces God and worship in a pure and free manner. It clearly differentiates itself from the more traditional style of worship, which paints an unwelcome picture for the hip-hop generation. Any time a group feels that they are not welcome, any open wounds are deepened and a gulf of missed ministry messages are blocked.

The major concern with this concept is that most churches that are labeled contemporary generally cater only to the youth and young adult generation. This develops a clear absence of seasoned or senior members. They, in turn, have the missing generation demographic found and highlighted in the traditional church. The middle ground must be filled.

The body of Christ was originally designed to be multi-generational on all levels. The church was founded and espoused on the concept of true unity, no matter what age or stage in life an individual finds themselves. The first and most primary unit in the scriptures is the family; the institution of family takes clear precedence even over the church itself.

The second established institution is the church. When an entire generation is absent or unwelcome within this premise, unity can and will not abound. The great theologian and professor of pastoral ministry, Gary L. McIntosh, states in his book, *One Church Four Generations*:

> *"There was a time not long ago when church leaders tried to minister to people as a single mass. No longer. Today's church leaders understand that ministry must take place among a mosaic of groups and subgroups-most notably generational cohorts."*

When the unique mixture and blend of generations occurs, a truly great benefit is experienced for all involved. This is truly a challenge to accomplish when each generation is separated in their 'own church'. It would be virtually impossible for young women to receive wisdom and godly nurturing from older, more mature Christian women when everyone that they share with is the same age. If the seasoned Christian never interacts with the younger one, successful ministry is never achieved.

This is an example of the generational divide and its effects. Both are detrimental to the growth of the church and the current generation's culture. Many of their fashion habits, attitudes, personalities, and issues are extensions of their lack of examples, mentors, wise counselors, and spiritual advisors. It is quite difficult to build a house, if you have never done so before. It is more of a challenge when there is not a blueprint, seasoned builder on site, or proper materials and tools to get the job done.

How can the church be the home where God's Spirit abides if it refuses to embrace those ewe lambs who simply seek guidance and lack direction? Paul speaks specifically to a generation of seasoned women regarding their younger counterparts:

> **Likewise, teach the older women to be reverent in the way they live, not to be slanderers or addicted to much wine, but to teach what is good. Then they can urge the younger women to love their husbands and children, to be self-controlled and pure, to be busy at home, to be kind, and to be subject to their husbands, so that no one will malign the word of God. Titus 2:3-5 (NIV)**

It is truly a challenge for a young person to learn to have a healthy relationship, to be slow to anger, to love God, and to be chaste in their sexuality and urges, if a wise individual from an earlier generation never teaches them how. If this kind of impartation never occurs, they will only attempt to develop their own rules, judgment, and understanding. This is the residual of the current culture of music and style. This generation cannot be overlooked or unwelcome due to our inability as Christian adults to serve the present age.

The multi-generational church will never return if the leaders of our traditional churches continue to use E. F. Hutton methods in a Mark Zukerburg society. The methods of the past, much like the technology, clothing, and concepts, are the reasons that staunchly traditional churches are rare.

During my childhood years, families came to church because it was a standard expectation. This was around the same time when mainstream church attendance began to decrease. In the decade of the 60s, younger parishioners attended church with their parents, because their parents believed and taught them that this was the right thing to do. A sense of obligation was a motivating factor for church attendance.

There were truly no ministries and activities that sought to gain and maintain membership back then. The nature of the times and its committed members assumed that the members would always be there. Therefore, minus Sunday school and a few annual events, churches did not have a structured or procedural retention plan.

When it came to the youth and young adults of this age, the actual workings and worship services of the church were not directed towards their needs and concerns. In addition, the youth rarely received an opportunity to feel that the church that they attended was theirs. As a result, many young people began to slowly and secretly harbor antagonistic feelings about the church and their future attendance. Numerous individuals within the "Buster Generation" have often verbalized the old adage: "When I grow up, I promise I'll never go to church again." Such statements indicate that even though they were made to come to church, the church was not ministering to them.

With the development of post-modernity and the questioning of church authority, traditions, and the institution itself, younger generations do not automatically accept the obligations and traditions that their parents and grandparents did. Many pastors have entered into traditional settings with the hopes of making their church more attractive to the younger generation, yet, when they tried to implement the changes, wholesale confusion erupted.

Even though their purpose was well-intentioned, their approach could have been a bit more welcoming and vision centered. The Apostle Paul, a great promoter of change, made healthy use of an accommodating spirit whenever he found it possible. Paul would always oppose *ungodly actions* head-on, regardless of the repercussions:

> **When Cephas came to Antioch, I opposed him to his face, because he stood condemned. For before certain men came ...he used to eat with the Gentiles. But when they arrived, he began to draw back and separate himself from the**

> *Gentiles because he was afraid of those who belonged to the circumcision group. The other Jews joined him in his hypocrisy...When I saw that they were not acting in line with the truth of the gospel, I said to Cephas in front of them all, "You are a Jew, yet you live like a Gentile and not like a Jew. How is it, then, that you force Gentiles to follow Jewish customs? Galatians 2:11-14 (NIV)*

However, in other situations which did not involve central issues of doctrine, Paul elected to operate in as inoffensive manner as possible. The principle of being accommodating and as sensitive as possible is important when trying to change the atmosphere of the traditional church.

Interestingly, most Christians have been taught that they are to place the needs of others before their own. In most case, many Christians believe and follow this precept. Unfortunately, when it comes to the worship experience and the way many parishioners "do" church, it is often "every Christian for him." Hence, what occurs are "worship wars."

This is where the traditional members have no tolerance for the younger members' style of worship and the younger members feel the same way about the traditional members' preferences. By no means am I under an illusion. Change is always challenging, even under the most ideal situations. Nevertheless, it's important that change in this particular area should and must be accomplished.

Did Hip Hop Kill Jesus?

I expect that many who read this are Christians. Also, I hope that people who are outside of the "spiritual ark of safety" will see this book as a progressive, positive, candid, and a clear interpolation of the viewpoints that can bring about much needed change. With the continual attempt to try and implement change, there must be an assertive effort to honor and acknowledge the past.

There are traditional ways and people that are having a positive impact on the church and the Zuckerburg generation. In the book, *The Soul of the Congregation*, there is a message that speaks extensively of honoring the E. F. Hutton ways. This must be understood in the midst of transition. The author, Dr. Thomas Edward Frank, promotes bringing balance to generational change and adaption. Dr. Frank makes a very interesting observation that is quite noteworthy:

> *For many laity this assumption leads to the conclusion that there must be another church someplace where 'they' know how to do 'church' better than 'we' do in this impossible little parish. What 'we' have here surely could not be 'church,' not with this leaky roof, squawking coir and dwindling membership."*

It is a balance that all individuals interested in making traditional churches more appealing to the youth desperately need. It must be highlighted that, even with its traditional and occasionally out-of-date ways, it is still the church. More importantly, it is the church that Jesus loves. Because some people are so intent upon not a mindset of change, but changing the church, they have a tendency to believe that their present church is not the real church, but will become the church when certain necessary changes are made.

I am not arguing that just because something is traditional it is inherently inferior, and thus, should be thrown away. I am, instead, attempting to implement changes that will honor and acknowledge all the traditional ways and people that still have a positive impact on the church. Yet, what a revelation it would be for traditional church worshippers to realize that God's call for love extends even to those who look and worship different than they do.

Yes, the church is called to show compassion toward the sick, the hungry and those in prisons, but what about the compassion and love that should be expressed toward younger Christian sisters and brothers in *their own worship service*? Conversely, the younger group should develop an appreciation of, and not disdain for, more traditional forms of worship. By doing so, they develop and promote a sense of balance, thereby embracing the wisdom and insight necessary for long term growth. This must always be the challenge that forces a successful resolution.

Regular church worshippers are not accustomed to thinking of how love should be expressed in the worship service. There is certainly an aspect of worship and church life that must be personal and portable.

If the traditional church desires that the younger generation return to the church, the traditional church must begin speaking the language of the Gospel According to Zuckerburg and slowly implement the teachings, beliefs, and concrete principles of Hutton.

If this concept and chain of communication is neglected, when God speaks, a lot of young people won't be listening!

CHAPTER FOUR

The Church Of Stipulations Minus God in Christ

Jonathan James is a bright and easy-going seventeen-year-old man living in an urban African-American community in Anywhere, U.S.A. Although he is clearly aware of the ills and ails of the violent inner city (i.e. drugs, gangs, unemployment, and teen pregnancy), so far he has been able to avoid these things. Fortunately, he has been raised by both of his parents and although his family is not wealthy, they have never suffered economically in the way that many of his friends have.

Jonathan's family is not religious; therefore attending church was never impressed upon him or his two younger brothers. He, along with his family, had a heightened sense of skepticism regarding the hypocritical perception of "church folks.". However, lately he has had strong and frequent nudging to know more about God. Perhaps, this could be categorized as just a natural maturing process, or, it could be due to the fact that he has experienced the death of several friends at an early age. Regardless of the reason for these new feelings, he has begun to question and wonder about the reason for it all.

Those who are evangelical Christians know that this young man is in a perfect position to hear about the gospel of Jesus Christ. Jonathan passes by a certain church every day on his way to school and one day decides that he would visit one on an upcoming Sunday to see what it is all about. The church that he chose to visit had been hailed by religious and civic societies as one of the gems of the city. It was an African-American Baptist congregation and one of the oldest churches in the city.

This church had a proud history. It stood on this particular corner for eighty years and had served a platform for proclaiming the gospel, aiding the community, helping to support the Civil Rights Movement, and as a strong denominational affiliate. Yet, when Jonathan came into the church on that Sunday, none of these things mattered to him.

The spiritual encounter highlights a desire to receive the wholeness of Christian ministry and connection with God. He came in with high expectations, but he left in discouragement. It was not that anyone was unkind to him; it was simply that everything he encountered was foreign. Not foreign in the sense of being unfamiliar, because he clearly realized that he was a first time visitor, yet it was foreign in the sense that nothing in the service spoke to his particular area of need.

He perceived that he could be a part of that particular ministry for 20 years and still not receive or feel anything. Here are a few reasons that Jonathan felt things were foreign to him were:

- ❖ Jonathan's attire resembled that of a typical young, urban young man, not a traditional churchgoer. In light of it, he received a few unwelcoming stares from older members that made him feel uncomfortable.

- ❖ The church was predominantly attended by people whose average age was forty years or more. This was not a major issue, yet, he thought there should have been some young people in attendance.

- ❖ He did not know or understand pattern or protocols concerning the order of service. He was not educated on the Sunday morning habits and rituals. He would have felt a little more comfortable if someone offered a few explanations as the service progressed.

- ❖ The music was an issue. He knew that there was great passion behind each song and he appreciated the sincerity, yet, it did nothing for him spiritually or emotionally.

- ❖ The final straw for Jonathan was the acknowledgment of the first time visitors. When the welcome was issued, they requested that all visitors stand so that they could acknowledge them. Jonathan did not want to stand, yet, all of the members in his vicinity knew that he was new and stared him down until he did so.

After roughly thirty minutes of this most unwelcoming and uncomfortable experience, Jonathan could not take anymore. He got up and left the building even before the minister stood in the pulpit to deliver the message.

Jonathan did not enter the church as an antagonist; he came in as an optimistic seeker desiring to be fulfilled. Unfortunately, he left church unfulfilled. This is the story of so many young people in the hip-hop generation. Often, they find themselves desirous of seeking God and salvation via the local church, yet, the stipulations and functions of the service and the unwelcoming nature of the congregation lead to journeys in futility.

This generation is teaching a class in sensitivity, education, and hospitality that their elders refuse to attend. Jonathan's comfort level dictated his attire. However, his attire had the unfortunate byproduct of making others within the church uncomfortable. They were unable to consider his internal desire: to know God.

There are so many stipulations within churches nationwide; yet, these stipulations are absent of spirituality and Christ-like principles. When this happens, the church is one that teaches Jesus but doesn't welcome the Spirit of Jesus. This paradox poses a major issue for young people. They will not attend events or facilities that do not carry out the principles that it supports. Therefore, many churches find the dominance of one particular age group or generation, which often eliminates the chance for new visitation or support.

The Church Of Stipulations Minus God in Christ

We discussed in Chapter One the universal language of music and its capacity to charm the soul. Yet, in the aforementioned example, the church's musical selections and choices were extremely foreign to Jonathan. With no one there to help him understand how the song selections applied to the order of service, and with no music that resonated with him, further disconnect was developed. When music is simply beneficial and germane to one particular generation, it limits the overall effectiveness. This reality forced the worship experience to become inconsequential to Jonathan and totally beneficial to its regular attendees only.

The uncomfortable issue that abounds in many churches more than the others is the pressure placed on those who desire to be anonymous. The "welcome" segment of the service is a great gesture; yet, the pressure-filled stares of the members do not align with their intent. Staring, with the purpose of placing an individual on the spot, does not support a comfortable atmosphere or a continuous desire for attendance. These disconnecting issues cause a divide that may never be filled.

Pastor Wannachange is the Senior Pastor of this traditional and well-regarded church. He is a thirty-three year old minister who has been there for only two years. Despite his seemingly happy and content appearance, an overwhelming sense of frustration has been brewing within.

When he was initially selected to pastor this ministry, he came with the hopes of making it more contemporary in its style and approach. Being thirty-one-years old at the time of his appointment, he could clearly see the need for bringing the church out of many of its traditional ways. In spite of the church's rich history and prominent local status, it was slowly dying due to its inability to adjust to the times.

The active membership was on a steady decline due to the deaths of many of its older members and the inability to replace these members with younger ones. Pastor Wannachange came in with the hopes of seeing things change for the better. Yet, as he began to implement the necessary changes, he faced great opposition from older and more settled members of the congregation. This push back caused the pastor great frustration.

This "Church of Stipulations Minus God in Christ" was so perturbed by the pastors desire to see change implemented that a mass number of underlying rumblings began to surface. Secret meetings between small groups began to surface in an effort to have the young minister voted out of the church. None of these rumors were ever made public or official, but the tension was seemingly unbearable.

This conflict of interest even caused church members who had once supported the vision of the pastor to either become a part of the opposition or leave the church altogether. Did he move too fast? Perhaps he was insensitive to the sentiments of the more seasoned members who had spent their entire lives at his church. Maybe the membership was simply too stuck in its own ways to embrace change.

Pastor Wannachange still ministers and preaches at the church weekly, yet, the fire within his soul has burned out. He rarely attempts any new things. His hope was to be a godly agent for change, a change that would bring youth and young adults to Christ, along with fresh ideas and youthful enthusiasm for the ministry. Despite this vision, he is simply a caretaker of traditions.

These fictional accounts vividly represent a real problem occurring all over our nation. In this hip-hop generation, so many young people want to find God. Many of them are seeking Him at locally established churches in their area. Also, there are change-minded ministers and church leaders who want to serve as catalyst for thorough change at these churches, but the two groups are rarely, if ever able to meet, due to the conflict that arises whenever changes are attempted.

There are so many Jonathans of all ages and genders, yet, they are being lost, discouraged, and misunderstood, because the church is full of stipulations minus God in Christ. Jonathan's soul is clearly at stake. Recognize that an alarming number of young people are both removing their emotion and changing their mentality when it relates to Christianity. More and more of the national population is progressively becoming immune to Christianity, particularly to the more traditional perspectives of the movement.

Congruently, a more critical and brashly verbal antagonist of the faith at large has arisen. With the current controversies and negative stigma often associated with the church, now more than ever, a rebellious attitude towards the church from the hip-hop and young adult generation grows at alarming rates. A great many members of this generation have taken the stance that they want no part of this thing called church.

Christians are viewed by this generation as consistently untrustworthy and factually inadequate. This viewpoint is fostered by the perception that the church and those who consider themselves Christians are hypocritical zealots who focus on the faults of others and rarely the wrongs of themselves.

We must come to grips with the fact that the young people's perception of the Christian experience has become clearly linked to the word "hypocrite." The Barna Research Group states that 85 percent of young outsiders have had sufficient exposure to Christians and churches, yet that they have concluded that present-day Christianity is hypocritical.

Oft times, Christians have been willing accomplices in portraying an unChrist-like disposition to non-believers. A percentage of young people who were once within the walls of the church have either felt unwelcome or turned off by the Christian portrayal of a false lifestyle. It is a lifestyle preaches a sermon it refuses to live. Others have chosen to create their own perception of what they view as the realities of churchgoers, based on what they have seen, heard, and concluded about Christ.

Regardless of this perception, many youth and young adults are not concerned about their perceptions of the church.

The Church Of Stipulations Minus God in Christ

Within their reality, they believe that people, of any belief or background, are not dependable; therefore, you should always expect to be disappointed by their actions. This perspective is not germane to the hypocritical rational, seeing that on some level they see that everyone is hypocritical. With this perspective, when Christians are hypocritical, it is really no big deal.

For youths, it is simply a matter of not practicing what is preached. Realistically, the Christian's lifestyle and point of view does not differ from the lifestyle and viewpoints of non-Christians.

Within this same data stream, you will find that roughly 30 percent of all professing born-again Christians in the United States admit to participating in viewing online pornography, some form of inappropriate behavior, or indulging in an inappropriate intimate sexual encounter out of wedlock. These statistics are in contrast to approximately 35 percent of all other Americans.

These concepts clearly connect to the examples that Jonathan experienced when he attempted to seek salvation at the church. He found that the skeptical and seemingly unwelcoming looks supported the hypocritical and unconcerned perceptions fostered by youth. These levels of biased perception must be eliminated and abandoned to allow Jesus to live past hip-hop.

The harsh reality is that much like music; the traditional church is out of tune with the hip-hop and young adult world.

Did Hip Hop Kill Jesus?

When you consider what marketers call brand identity, you will often think of long standing brands like Coca-Cola, McDonald's, Starbucks, Wal-Mart, and Apple. When you consider what each of these brands mean to people, it could range from words like refreshing, dependable, number one, or competitive pricing. Yet, when you ask people what they consider about the image and 'brand' of Christianity, opinions differ. People use analogies like:

An organization on the verge of collapse.

The blind leading the blind.

An ostrich with its head in the sand.

No matter how you say it, these thoughts foster the belief that Christianity is out of touch and unconcerned about it. With the average non-believer not clearly understanding the role of the church in society and within their own lives, they find it difficult to believe in Christianity. Despite this, many youths still believe that an exercised faith assists people in living a stronger, more abundant life.

Nevertheless, many participants in the hip-hop generation believe that Christianity is confusing and a bit overwhelming. Being a follower of Jesus Christ is no longer in sync with the fast paced, ever changing world in which we now live. With the reputation of being out of tune and inadequate, Christianity is facing rebranding as outdated and prehistoric.

It is so easy, with Jonathan's experience and others, to believe that Christians are living in a world unique only to themselves. They are speaking, seeing, and operating with effects that even they don't understand. They continually isolate themselves from the realities, issues, and struggles of the real world, thereby, eliminating the growth, change, and salvation of the real world.

Is it possible for the church to start playing in a key that soothes the ills and ails of the people, or will this once powerful vessel find itself sinking into the dark, murky waters of uselessness?

This organism will not continue to live without learning a few vital lessons from the youth and generation that they seemingly try so hard to reject. Music is only beautiful when harmony is experienced, yet, without allowing for the diversity of different genres and interpretations of the song, the notes and melody tend to be irrelevant and ineffective.

> *Is it possible to be the Church without Jesus Christ?*
>
> *Can the message be delivered if the mailing address is incorrect?*
>
> *Can the church honestly afford to remain the same while dying from stagnation?*

Jonathan and so many like him are seeking to find Jesus and His salvation. Pastor Wannachange is being muzzled and burned out because of aggressive traditionalism and unwarranted fear. This generation must be embraced and the church must become relevant again. Its brand is tarnished, yet, it refuses to rebuild in order to become powerful in the eyes of the consumer.

The church has an open door that welcomes with open arms, as long as Jesus is glorified and our fears and traditionalism is minimized.

CHAPTER FIVE

We Worship Better Together

There are certain changes that must be made to the way church operates worship services and ministries. These changes will make church more attractive to young people, and in turn, transform them into fully integrated members of church life. This may sound like a broad statement, but it works. Our church, in particular, faced a scarcity of youth. Even facing this, our work was successful.

At the beginning of our mammoth project, some young people were attending, yet the numbers were extremely low. I had been pastoring this same church for 17 years, and I, much like Pastor Wannachange, was well aware of the need for a more youthful presence and participation. Even though I knew the numbers were down, for the purpose of research and statistical data, I had two of my associates observe both of our Sunday morning services. Each service has a unique personality and feel, thereby, providing us with a different dynamic.

Did Hip Hop Kill Jesus?

In the early years of my pastorate, from 1989 until the mid-nineties, the church grew rapidly and youths regularly attended. I was called to this ministry at the ripe old age of thirty-three. I was not called to pastor one particular generation, yet, my accommodating and kind-hearted nature resonated with the youth. They saw that I was neither a pushover, nor easily prone to anger. To understand the dynamics of my experience, you must have a picture of my personal ministry.

The church that I pastor has been in existence for 66 years. Located in the inner city on the east side of Cleveland, Ohio, the church stands on a busy thoroughfare, connecting the east and west sections of the city. The nearby residents range from middle to lower middle class, with an approximately 30% of residents who are indigent. The community has a total population of 25,348 residents, with 12,028 males (47.5%) and 13,320 females (52.5%). The median age is 32.5 years old. Those 65 years and over make up 13% of the population, while 67.7% of the population house those 18 years and over.

Although the median age is quite young, the church's demographics did not reflect this. Most of the members of the church commute from nearby suburbs and communities. With nearly 9,500 individuals in this community below the poverty level, it is part of a larger city heralded as among the poorest in America. This particular aspect of statistical data is important because it does not matter whether your situation is extremely wealthy or on the lower tiers of economic struggle, you can transition your ministry into generationally diverse context.

With these statistics as a backdrop, I have been privileged to lead some of the greatest and most passionate people in the world. Yet, even after seventeen years, I found that I had not quite "jelled" with a number of the traditional things, which occurred in the church. I entered into the business of making small changes wherever necessary, over the course of several years. During the course of these constant changes, the things that were clearly wrong begin to stop almost instantly. Despite these purposeful changes, I found myself dealing with an abundance of the transitionally neutral "we have always done it this way" Christians.

The older members are amazingly comfortable with traditionalism; yet, this comfort level has increasingly made the younger people more uncomfortable. As alluded to earlier, there was truly a desire in my heart to foster a strong ministry for the youth, yet, never isolate a particular generation. This is not about being youthful, as much as it is about being cognizant that youthfulness is a major factor for the life of any ministry.

That period left an indelible impression in my mind as it relates to my Christian walk. Although I had given my life to Christ at an early age, my initial adult years were when my true ministry work began. I vividly remember the joys and heartbreaks of church life that I experienced as a young adult. It was both bitter and beneficial, and my passion to minister to young people at such a pivotal time in their lives is and should be the churches central focus.

The church should effectively evangelize to the needs of this and every generation. This should stand as a key characteristic. This is one of the primary purposes of our faith. Quite simply, young people are not participating in church in large numbers. During the most active and energetic years of their lives, when they are growing, maturing, raising children, establishing careers, and enjoying good health, they are not in church. One generation is worshiping apart from another.

We worship better together; yet, we consistently fail to do so. Seeing that the church's traditional style no longer appeals to the youthful pallet, many who do not go on to contemporary churches usually seek no spiritual direction at all.

We must focus on establishing a plethora of multi-generational churches, with ministries for all age groups, thereby bringing this generation to fellowship and blessing their lives in turn.

I have found that many individuals, particularly in the African-American community, grew up participating in church. Once they reached adulthood, large portions of these individuals ceased to attend. With the establishment of holistic ministry and the effective embrace of each generation, there is an opportunity to regain their attendance. I recognize that some days I awaken and feel cool, trendy, and wedged firmly within the culture of hip-hop. Yet, age can often promote a perception of separation that can easily be translated as an utter and distinct disconnection from the youthful reality.

What then must a church and culture do when one generation is operating millions of miles away from another?

This is the point when we must forge solid and valuable relationships with one another. You must make practical steps to open your mind and life up to things that seem foreign, to people who are not frequent visitors of your community of faith, and by extending your circle of influence. We must bridge the gap that separates our lives on every level.

With the advent of the World Wide Web, television, and around the clock news, there is no excuse for maintaining relevance and freshness at any age or stage of life.

The Barna Group provides the statistic that eight out of ten students are actively engaged in a church during the teen years. Shockingly, a vast majority of them will make a calculated and permanent exit from any form of active spirituality or faith by the time they reach eighteen.

They perceive that their once active faith is now antiquated, irrelevant, and lack luster. Instead of continuing in the habit of simply trying to stimulate their minds, we must effectively start embracing and impacting their lives. Even though most of our change has been focused on adjusting how we do church, almost none of these attempts have impacted the image of church in a positive manner.

There is an extremely small window of time by which we can reach teenagers to help them to see church and Christ as more than simply a committed activity. If we do not allow young people to engage the church at a hands-on level, we run the risk of losing them on all levels.

How much better would the lives of our youths be, if they receive the fellowship and nurturing of the church in childhood, teenage, middle age, and during their senior years? It would be wonderful to have an unbroken chain of spiritual growth that reinvents itself with every generation. How beneficial is their journey when Christ is seen as a *lifelong* partner? This is an amazingly crucial age, and the church, as an attractive and appealing place with a wonderful mixture of age groups, can be such an asset to their lives.

Another targeted group within this generation is those who are heavily involved in the raising and nurturing of their children. Hence, bringing these young people back into the church will impact others within this generation accordingly. Recognize that in most church environments, getting the smaller children is not the problem; nevertheless, many churches are ineffective in their ability to attract this market.

Their parents are the key. They are more than willing to follow their parents, in the event that their parents are willing to come. We must creatively and effectively consider a type of at-home evangelism. It is not evangelism in the sense of missionaries and evangelist going out to bring people in. This evangelism focuses on effective internal ministry that once practiced successfully at home will encourage others to follow suit.

The Apostle Paul admonished the Corinthians because of their misuse of spiritual gifts, which made them appear "crazy" to non-believers who might have been desirous of coming to worship. He told them that they should worship in such a way that the non-believers who happen to attend would be convicted of the truth of Christianity. This is truly 'at home' evangelism.

To assist my church in worshipping better together, I created an intervention project with three steps. On the first Sunday, I informed my congregation of what the project was about and of the need for some willing participants who would serve as interview subjects for church growth. I needed individuals who were at least 40 years of age and supportive of the projects idea. In turn, I chose 5 young people within our church, which were between the ages of 13 to 18, to complete a questionnaire to find out what changes they would like to see occur at the church. These changes would ultimately attract others of comparable age.

Finally, I decided to select a group of seasoned members in positions of authority and influence to be a sample group. They would receive four customized lessons on the importance of change. This change would be a key component in attracting youth to our church.

On the first Sunday of the project, I informed the congregation about this endeavor and outlined my heart's desire to make the church more appealing and attractive to young people overall. This would be effectively accomplished by attempting to maintain the church's unique traditional flavor. By no means was I attempting to transform the church into a contemporary church, but I did desire to cultivate their awareness of the changes necessary to redirect our focus to young people and their salvation.

I was intrigued to find, on a grassroots level, exactly how each sector of the church felt about moving towards a place that ministered to all on a multi-generational level. Many may find it strange to interview older members when younger ones are whom we are attempting to attract. Yet, to make this transition effective, everyone must be made to feel as though they are a part of the change.

The project was not just about making changes, but about encouraging changes in a loving manner, a manner which considered those who were already members and those that we were endeavoring to attract. There was an unexpected benefit from engaging the traditionalist first. It is one that I will highlight in detail in later chapters.

Effectively, traditionalist and the young adult generation must both be participants of this change. Without a unified effort, no change will be experienced. Know that there should always be the incorporation of "we" and not simply "them" or "us." The senior members in any church are important and key components in this change, particularly due to their wisdom and insight. They must recognize how important they are in the change process. We ALL worship better together and without us ALL, the change is limited in its effectiveness.

I encourage each reader to focus on changing together, so that your ministries and generations will not continue to fall apart.

CHAPTER SIX

Out of the Mouths of Babes

Although we are more than halfway through this book, this book is now truly beginning.

The hip-hop generation of non-Christians is verbalizing specific criticisms of the faith and of the people, as well. Merely recognizing and prescribing a remedy for the issue are only starting points. Obvious questions have arisen. How do we address the issues? What can be done to alter the hip-hop generation's viewpoint of our faith?

My honest prayer is that this book initiates dialogue regarding the state of the church's reputation in the eyes of our youth and in our culture overall. Whether you embrace the concepts of this book or reject them, there are complicated and volatile concerns that have been raised, many of which are visible, and others, which hide underneath the skin. We must challenge these concerns, and the hip-hop generation, through our own efforts of correction. By doing so, we work towards making the message of Christ welcoming to all.

When accessing the youth and young adult mindset, the focus on how to arrive at a particular destination is often more important than the destination. There must be a focus on the steps to help them focus on the destination.

Secondly, understand that what you do is more important than what you say. As you recall the concept of hypocrisy, you'll remember that it is important to the hip-hop generation to walk what you talk. We must embrace a more cautious point of view to impact their perception of faith and salvation. With this in mind, implementing the pushy and aggressive concept regarding faith can cause an extreme sense of reluctance. There must be a heightened sense of attention that is relevant for success.

This highlights the lessened chance that the hip-hop Christians will be evangelical in sharing their faith in Christ with others, as opposed to the more seasoned Christians being moved to share Christ with others. This generation's concept of a truly meaningful life does not necessarily include a relationship with Christ.

Furthermore, there is an increasingly diminished belief in the "eternal security of the believer" concept that a committed relationship with Jesus Christ is the factor that secures one's post mortal afterlife. This foundational belief cannot be reached, if the clarity of true relationship is developed. It is much like discussing a 45-year wedding anniversary without establishing the basic concepts of love, respect, and communication while dating. The theological premise is important, but the relational concepts are important to the development of this generation, too.

As it relates to relational aspects, one of the greater viewpoints that must be overcome with this generation is a focus on pure goodness. The segments of this generation that are not a part of the Body of Christ, in general, do not hold the belief that the motives of Christians, when attempting to evangelize them towards conversion, are founded in goodness.

There is a lack of belief, when discussing these topics with young people, that Christians have a pure concern for non-Christians as people. They believe that they are simply perceived as another notch on the salvation belt, as opposed to concerned for them as humans. This is an area that causes a major divide: the majority of Christians truly believed that they come across to non-believers as genuine; nevertheless, the non-believing young generation categorically refutes this point.

Regardless of the fact that our soul-winning mission is genuine to us, many of today's youth feel like a bull's eye with Christians as the darts. They believe that us Christians are out to fill our churches with members, or, to add another medallion to our "who I saved this week" jacket. During our delivery, somehow the mail gets lost and never makes it to the proper destination.

Somehow, we must begin to listen to the youth and understand that no matter how we feel about the message or how many times the method has been successful, if it ceases to reach the masses any longer, the mission will be unsuccessful.

Let me help to bring validity to the voice of the hip-hop generation with a larger base of statistics. The Barna Research Group has done research to support this perspective:

> *"Only one out of seven outsiders describes Christianity as something that seems genuine and real. Just one-third believe that Christians show genuine interest in them...Most outsiders have grown up around Christians, many have given the "Jesus thing" a thorough test drive; a majority have tried churches and found them desperately lacking relevance...Most young people have already formed their conclusions about Christianity. These people have heard about Jesus, they can recite concepts and stories found in the Bible, and they believe they pretty much 'get it.' It is a daunting task to break through people's preconceptions when they think they've seen the movie before."*

WOW! This is the stuff we must discuss. These are the thoughts that come directly from the mouths of this generation. We cannot continue to perceive a situation as we desire without honestly evaluating the feedback of the people we are attempting to target. When using the concept of marketing in the business world as an example, it is utterly impossible for a company to promote a product that people need when the sales team comes over to the mass majority of clients as generic and robotic.

When marketing research is performed and the survey results state that the focus group feels the company cares only about their purchase power, instead of them as a client, conflict arises. It begs the question of whether the business owner should stay focused on past successes and the traditional market base, or attempt to focus on this new, relevant, and valuable market.

If you understand this from a business perspective, and would be willing to make a major adjustment to make sure the target market is appreciated and valued, how can the church hear the concerns of youth and dismiss them as invalid, biased, or unworthy of adjustment? We must begin to bring awareness and a readily adjustable mindset to the table of traditional Christianity.

The Bible is concise regarding the first steps to the Christian journey of faith:

> *The he said, "Jesus, remember me when you come into your kingdom." Jesus answered him, "Truly I tell you, today you will be with me in paradise." Luke 23:42-43 (NIV)*

When pointing out one of the concerns of this generation, how is it possible that discipleship is substituted or eliminated? Otherwise, the argument can arise that non-believers are receiving the message that following Christ is simply about the conversion of your salvation. We rarely, if at all, deliver the message that this is a lifestyle change by which you have now enrolled into being a member of the Kingdom of God and a member of the body of Christ, now, henceforth, and forever more. This transition is one that will impact every inch and space of your life from this point forward.

With this being clear, the miscommunication is that most Christians believe they have explained this concept to non-believers with the same level of clarity. If we are doing this, why is it that such a major portion of the focus ministry is failing to get the message? Why are we losing the connection with youth if we are honestly making a connection? In this culture of evangelical disconnect, the converted believers in the target market fall into the abandoned believers or convenient Christian category.

To conjure the perception we desire, that of being concerned not just about conversion, but about the individual as well, it is essential that we become well balanced in our portrayal of what it truly means to be a follower of Christ. We must immediately begin to re-brand and repackage our message to the youthful masses. We must start focusing our attention on inward spiritual transformation.

When attempting to define inward spiritual transformation, it can be quite challenging to determine what it is, or more importantly, how it looks. The challenge that must be overcome is the belief that we are all about assimilation. Assimilation is defined by Rick Warren as:

> *"The task of moving people from an awareness of your church to active membership and participation in your church."*

We must focus on the in-depth, ingrained passion that should govern one's life and walk as a follower of Jesus Christ. If we are able to pinpoint an outcome and a process by which this concept is beneficial and rewarding, we can overcome this negative perception. This concept should develop a new way of listening, a more sincere way of loving, and a clearer way of thinking.

A new way of listening involves a pinpointed focus for a transformation in the spirit. This will provide ability for an individual to listen not simply for God's direction, but for the natural enhancement necessary to hear the messages of others more clearly. As a pastor and leader, I have found that when dealing with the concerns and needs of others, the ability to have a compassionate heart is the result of being able to listen. When you are able to listen to the voice of God, whether through supplication, prayer, fasting, reading His Word, hard times, or relationships, the listening ability has been enhanced through true connection with Him.

Being able to hear what He is saying in this age over and against what He was saying in the past is what prompts me to focus on guiding the church to embrace the hip-hop generation. Without the ability to listen, we will continue to foster loss and encourage disconnect because we have been unable to embrace spiritual transformation through listening. When Christians can relay this message with a sincere heart, young people can receive it not simply as a conversion scheme, but as a clear desire for God's people to see others made better along their daily journey.

Second, a more sincere way of loving must be displayed if we desire to be transformational in our faith and fellowship to believers and non-believers alike, no matter their age, color, gender, or denomination. When we focus on this attribute, who, what, where, why, and how we do things for and towards will change drastically. Furthermore, others will easily see it. When we see that the scriptures define God as love, yet, we overlook the opportunity to exonerate love in evangelism, how are we followers of the Most High?

Jesus states in the Gospel of Mark:

> **The most important one, answered Jesus, is this: Hear, O Israel: The Lord our God, the Lord is one. Love the Lord your God with all your heart and with all your soul and with all your mind and with all your strength. The second is this: Love your neighbor as yourself. There is no commandment greater than these. Mark 12:29-31 (NIV)**

Please recognize that one's belief in God does not necessarily make a person loving. This is something that must be worked towards on the Christian journey, so that other non-Christians can feel the love. It can no longer be solo, consumption focused point of view. There must be a clear transition. We must begin to embrace the type of love outlined in the scriptures, so that we will be able to love our neighbor as ourselves. This is a process of growth, not an automatic movement of the heart.

When we learn to embrace this concept, transformation of perspective will engulf the non-Christian hip-hop generation and encourage them to seek God, based on the love that overflows from believers to them.

Finally, a clearer way of thinking must permeate our thoughts and actions. The Book of Proverbs 23:7 states that as a man thinks in his heart, so is he. This concept seems physiologically impossible because there is no ability for the heart to think. Yet, the writer of the Proverbs is clearly making a connection between the psychology, cardiology, and anthropology of a human.

The phrase "as a man thinks," from a symbolic standpoint, highlights a person's psychology, and refers to a mental process which promotes a response from the heart. Next, when the feelings and emotions of the heart are involved, a person's cardiology is effected. Once it is birthed in the mind and transferred to the heart via emotions and feelings, an action is carried out in your being, anthropology. You become and act on what you think first, in your mind.

Therefore, an inward transformation of the way one thinks must be changed. This requires a daily state of mental metamorphosis. This is outlined in Romans 12:2 (NIV):

> ***Do not conform to the pattern of this world,***
> ***but be transformed by the renewing of your***
> ***mind.***

This highlights the focus of not thinking as the world would have you think, but developing a clear spiritual thought process, thereby, changing your entire physiological makeup. One of the major disconnects in ministry lies in the inability to convey to the youth the psychological steps necessary to produce viable fruit. Overlooking this concept continues to support the traditional mindset, thereby no longer transforming the congregation or welcoming the hip-hop generation.

We, as Christians, cannot continue to develop a universal message that implodes with the lack of connectivity to the customized and unique concerns, issues, and personalities of today's youth. The hip-hop generation desires and needs to be enriched regarding the truths of God and the challenges of their daily lives. Learning to think will help bridge this divide.

These are the items that must be attended to, thereby bringing symmetry to a relationship that has drifted off course. This generation possesses the willingness to be a part of the church, yet the church must meet their willingness with true ministry. Would you continue to patronize a restaurant that prepared food only one menu item? You visited the establishment in the past and can remember a tasty, versatile menu, yet, when you visit nowadays, the only thing on the menu is lima beans.

I do recognize that lima beans are healthy, good for the digestive system, and otherwise beneficial from a nutritional standpoint, but are insufficient to encourage a continual patronage to a restaurant. With the option of a few different meats, additional sides, and beverage selections, the occasional order of lima beans may not be so bad. Please recognize that lima beans alone are not sufficient, in and of themselves, for a healthy diet.

We must begin to listen to the concerns of this generation in our churches and Christian traditionalism. Many in this generation want to eat from our "restaurant;" however, we offer too few selections.

No matter how good the beans are, versatility still benefits everyone. Therefore, listen to the concerns and grow from them.

CHAPTER SEVEN

The Do Something Experience

If you have spent any time recently with a person in their teens or early twenties, you will quickly recognize that they are all about action and that they want action now. This generation does not believe in the mindset of delayed gratification, yet, they live every day, in the words of the hip-hop artist Rocko, "like it's no tomorrow." Therefore, a confined and tentative faith is clearly out of sync with the aggressive mindsets and issues that confront the youths of this generation.

Consider this:

- ❖ This generation has developed in an ever-changing, social environment which is increasingly more aggressive than that of their parents or grandparents. Crime rates are triple those of the period from the 1950s to the 1980s and crimes of an extremely violent nature have quadrupled in number since that time. This type of shameless violence hampers the safety of young people all across this country.

77

- ❖ The structure of the family has experienced an overwhelming change in the last thirty years. More than 33% of all babies born in the US are children of unwed parents. In many American metropolis areas, approximately 66% of all children are born into unwed families.

- ❖ Less than 1/3rd of young people approved of pre-marital sex by the end of the 1950s, yet, now more than 2/3rds approve of it. This is a mirror image of the current lifestyle, attitude, and culture of this present age.

- ❖ Profane and inappropriate language is the norm as it relates to communication and personal expression.

- ❖ At least one out of seven young adults has dealt with some form of depression. Thirty-three percent are obese or suffer from weight-related addictions. One out of every six is in serious debt. Approximately 20% of all married young adults have already experienced divorce.

- ❖ One out of every eight young adults are lonely. Approximately half of young adults say they are attempting to develop good friendships. Twenty-five percent of young adults feel unfulfilled in their careers. Almost half of young adults in America state that they are stressed.

- ❖ Suicide is among the top five leading causes of death among young people ages fifteen to twenty-four. In the mid-2000s, 1 out of 6 high school students in the US have contemplated suicide during the current year.

I can continually provide supporting statistics regarding why it is imperative for those of us, within the Christian community to embrace this generation. The hip-hop generation cannot afford for us to live in our box of traditionalism. We must go to where they are and engage them on their level.

When I endeavored to initiate change within my own church, I constantly reminded my congregation that we were only focusing on changing areas not related to clear biblical doctrines and teachings. It is important for you to understand that the challenge of changing a traditional church must highlight adjustments to the areas of traditionalism that have nothing to do with biblical truths or precepts. The changes focus on concepts that we, as people have developed in our personal context that are generally not rooted in biblical truths. The change areas are not relevant to concepts that are sound and true within the Bible. This must be made clear.

The challenge is that many traditionalists feel as if their traditions are sanctioned by the bible and that deviation is a sin. It is clear that we must teach, even more definitively, how the congregation should make a distinction between biblical requirements and human traditions.

One of the easiest and best ways to implement change in a church setting is to offer a companion ministry or activity. These are concepts which can be developed alongside the present ministry, instead of completely stopping the present way things are carried out. With this process, the members have an option of how they want to do a certain ministry activity.

This companion ministry cannot be used in every situation. Yet, some situations may need to be eliminated for the betterment of growth and revenue; nonetheless, it can be a peaceful transitional approach for changing ministry.

Another area where the companion technique can be used is when individuals are participating in the Invitation to Discipleship at the end of service. This is an appeal for non-member and non-Christians to come forth and join the local church body. Within the culture of the African-American church, this appeal is usually extended at the end of every church service. It is informally referred to as "opening the doors of the church." This is a public act. Within the context of my research, it has been found that people today, especially young people, are more reluctant to come forward and join in a public fashion.

Although their culture is one of immediacy, the comfort level of youths' does not always mirror as much. Knowing this, I altered the normal process of invitation to include the opportunity for anyone desirous of joining the church to have that opportunity after church services. This can be done in the privacy of the pastoral offices for their convenience. There should be no excuse for missing an opportunity to accept Christ as your Savior.

There are several parallel ways to accomplish change, yet, change must be embraced. Consider surgery, a medically invasive technique done only when absolutely necessary. Usually during surgery, something in the body is cut out, or, the body is cut open. However, if an effective medicine, technique, or therapy can be administered to the body, then the same goal could be achieved with less trauma to the body.

In the church, the people interested in making changes should perform spiritual "surgery" only when necessary. When something else can be added or taken away, it can mean less "trauma" or conflict for the church.

One area where great aid regarding this matter can be found by gleaning from the conversations and interactions of senior members. Although this may come as a surprise to some, this involves the continual and purposeful honoring of the church heroes of the past. One of the things that will be consistently uncovered in speaking with the older members is their natural love and desire to reminisce about the past.

This is the reality of any church, organization, or business with senior or seasoned members. It is a well-known fact that people have a tendency to romanticize the past, especially when present situations are not to their personal liking. This is evident even in scripture. The recently freed Jews in the book of Exodus, after being freed only a few short days, began to daydream about their misery in Egypt, only because things appeared to be going bad in the desert:

> *In the desert the whole community grumbled against Moses and Aaron. The Israelites said to them, "If only we had died by the Lord's hand in Egypt! There we sat around pots of meat and ate all the food we wanted, but you have brought us out into this desert to starve this entire assembly to death."*
> *Exodus 16:2-3 (NIV)*

Even ineffective pastors who have passed away often become great pastors when a present pastor is not liked. The present pastor who is attempting changes may encounter opposition because of this fondness that the older members have with the past. One way to mitigate this issue may be to continually honor and speak well of past significant persons and past significant things. The natural tendency might be to ignore the past.

Nevertheless, I would like to suggest that the leaders who are involved in change honor the past. Whenever the pastor can honor a past achievement or person, while simultaneously trying new things, it will help to bring changes about more peacefully.

As you begin to do something to implement change, here are a few things you should remember for a traditional church to become more appealing to youth in as loving a manner as possible:

- ❖ Change must always begin at the top. The pastor is the first advocate for change. He or she must first be convinced of the biblical justification for change.

This will help support and sustain the leader when opposition occurs. The pastor must be convinced that if a whole section of the community is missing, there is a problem and the problem must be addressed. Because the context is a traditional one, pastors must also be convinced that they must be the agent for necessary changes, done as lovingly as possible. If the conflict is to come, and it will, it should be because someone simply does not like what the pastor does, not how the pastor did it.

- ❖ The best way to start is to educate this congregation, biblically, on the need for changes. They must be educated on the problem. They must recognize that traditions are not on par with the Bible. They must be reminded of the importance of meeting individuals where they are and bringing them where God wants them to be. The church is never to compromise biblical truths, but instead, to make adjustments as far as traditions are concerned, so as to be relevant to the hip-hop generation today.

- ❖ Even after educating the church on the need for changes, it's important to make a concerted effort to get key members of the church on board with the changes. Talk with them, have special sessions with them, take them to lunch, etc. Keep your ideas before them. This will keep them aware of what's occurring and help them feel included. They will be less apt to oppose change.

- ❖ Find out from both groups (older/traditionalists and the younger members who are there) exactly what changes they want. This is where the pastor can get added ideas on exactly what changes to make. This will also help the congregation to feel as if they are a part of the process.

- ❖ Prayerfully examine suggestions given, and the changes that the pastor personally may have, to see the feasibility of each. When it is clear that a change must occur, make the change. Whenever possible, add a new ministry rather than cut out something old. When something absolutely must be cut out, explain why, but proceed forward!

- ❖ In every area, place the right people in the right positions. In all instances, encourage leaders and all who work in the church to be excellent in everything they do.

- ❖ Finally, realize that this should be an ongoing process. Always be on the lookout for ways to improve the relevancy of the church to the community. Always seek to place yourself in the shoes of a new person who is visiting the church. This should be reflected in the preaching style, the songs that are sung and in all ministry activities. Learn to always meet people where they are.

This is what the "do something" experience is all about. It cannot be accomplished unless you actually DO

SOMETHING. This generation is depending on your ministry, your leadership, and your vision. Every individual can experience Jesus in this generation if you just Do the Something you have been called to do!

Hip-Hop is waiting on the Jesus in you to get up and wave your change in the air!

CHAPTER EIGHT

Plenty Good Room

I have been engaging in a number of small changes, and some not so small changes, during my seventeen years of pastoring. However, this ministry transition assisted me in pastoring in a focused and comprehensive way as I cued in on the best ways to help my church accomplish lofty, yet necessary goals.

As outlined in Chapter Five, when every response was received from the interviews of the over-forty group, the questionnaires from the youth were compiled, the responses and comments from the sample group were likewise compiled, and the information from my personal journal was chronicled. The result was that an amazing change was implemented within our ministry, prompting me to write this wonderful book.

Please understand that I was not immediately able to implement all of the suggestions in the surveys, but many of them were utilized expediently. In addition, several others were developed and rolled out as appropriate. Part of my success was found in the ability to understand that my congregation would accept changes gradually. These changes were a bright light to shine in our community, city, and ultimately, our state. Realize that when there are drastic changes being made of this magnitude, you must implement them with a sense of systematic progression, not abruptly.

There is an art to change. It cannot be implemented too soon or too fast. In the best case scenario, the traditionalists would love changes, provided they were carried out properly. At worst, they would respectfully tolerate it or exit due to displeasure. Often, change will not satisfy everyone involved, so you must take this into consideration. The change that we implemented within the first three months of transition resulted in moderate, yet, noticeable improvements. It clearly appeared that this change was working!

During the first phase of implementation, a total of 38 new people received Christ and joined our church. Included in this number were three families:

Fifteen were over the age of 40.

Twenty-three were under the age of 40.

Furthermore:

Five of the 23 were in their 20s.

Six of the 23 were in their 30s.

Eight of the 23 were teenagers.

Four of the 23 were pre-teens.

Overall, 60% of the new members were under the age of 40. Forty percent were over the age of 40.

Prior to this project, individuals were joining at an average rate of roughly 3 to 5 people per month. Therefore, this was a tremendous upswing within our church and community. It was also clear that the young people who were joining were becoming active in at least one ministry more readily than in the past. The youth activities went on to have an average participation of roughly 15 to 20 youths, whereas in the past, they averaged 8 to 10. These numbers are a great indicator of progress from prior years when very few young people were joining.

When it came down to the mood and attitude of the parishioners since this transition occurred, the change was also gradual. The group, as a whole, did not exhibit much change in their perspectives, but questionnaires indicated that they favored greater youth participation in the church. However, the majority of the sample group indicated that they would have problems if certain traditions were changed.

The congregation, as opposed to the sample group, had a totally different view. In contrast, they portrayed a livelier spirit of acceptance. The church noticed the upswing in people joining and that the younger people were more attentive and, at times, quite involved.

There is indeed a new spirit in the church. I have not heard as much criticism regarding the changes from older or more traditional members. With the implementation of sermons and classes regarding change, along with the comprehensive inclusion of all members from the projects inception, the accepting spirit of new things has served as a welcoming atmosphere engaging all, including young people in the hip-hop culture who are more likely to visit and return for the worship experience.

Every traditional member can see the results of this project. People are joining right before their eyes. I believe that the desire to change has done so much to heighten awareness for the traditionalists regarding the imminent need for change. Thankfully, it has worked! The people now expect changes in our ministry, and subconsciously, in their own lives.

Many members have even begun to take an inquisitive, proactive attitude, showing interest in the changes that are to come. Whether statements like this are viewed as hopeful expectancy or simple pessimism, there is nonetheless an awareness that the winds of change are aggressively blowing. When the changes do occur, they are not caught off guard. Furthermore, it is assumed that my track record for implementing successful change would put them at ease.

Pastoring these wonderful people has helped me understand the personality and precepts of this church. This insight provided me with an understanding of the past to keenly calculate changes that are beneficial and noteworthy over and against those that should be tabled for another time. I am no longer concerned with angry groups developing a confrontational demeanor about certain aspects of change.

Traditional members are no longer in an uproar when a young person who joins is not dressed to their liking. Although the traditional members would definitively prefer that they dress in a more traditional way, they are no longer as vociferous in their reactions. As changes continue to be made, the church has taken on a more accepting spirit. Helping you find this accepting spirit in your church is the major goal of this book.

A pastor was once called to a small church and had been there for roughly three weeks. He preached diligently for the first few Sundays. As he did so, he stood near an eye sore of a piano in the front of the sanctuary. The piano was unable to be played because of its diminished state and advanced age. It had been donated several years prior by a well-respected pioneer in the church and community. This gentleman died before the pastor arrived, therefore the piano served as a sentimental memory in the hearts of this small congregation. The new pastor was unaware of the piano's history and was growing weary of the look the piano gave the sanctuary.

On the fourth Sunday of his pastorate, he demanded that the piano be moved from the sanctuary, effective immediately. On Monday morning, the trustees of this small church met to relieve the new pastor of his leadership duties, also effective immediately. The pastor was shocked and disappointed, yet, he heeded their request.

About three years later, the former pastor was in town and decided to visit his old church. When he came within blocks of the adjacent street, he noticed cars parked on both sides of the street for miles. The service was jubilant and the church was filled to capacity. As he observed the service from the back of the sanctuary, he noticed that the piano was no longer in the building. Furthermore, a pianist played a beautiful baby grand.

At the end of the service, the former pastor approached the current pastor in a huff. He demanded to know about the amazing church growth, the jubilant service, and most importantly, the removal of the ugly piano.

"How did you get these people to remove the old piano?" the irate pastor demanded.

"Oh," the current pastor replied. "That was the easy part. You tried to move the piano in a day. I moved it an inch at a time."

I do not wish to paint an unrealistic picture, arguing that what happened at my church will happen the exact same way everywhere. Just as people are unique, churches are in turn unique, and will progress at their own rate. It is upon pastors, however, to ensure that they do. The increase in membership and the absence of hostilities in my instance have demonstrated that progress can be made, but that it takes time.

This type of change is necessary, so that a culture does not kill Jesus by way of our traditional, self-centered, and unwilling ways. We can learn so much from the hip hop generation, and in turn, they can and are willing to learn a lot from us.

There is no better time to change than now. There is plenty of room in your ministry, life, community, and heart for Jesus to make just such a change.

Therefore, there is only one question.

Will you let Him?

References

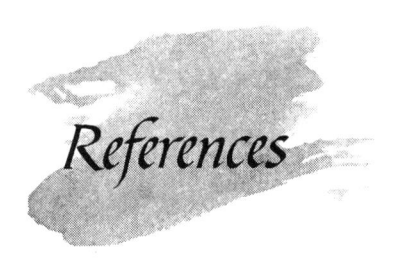

Badelle, George C.; Sandon, Leo Jr.; Wellborn, Charles T. (1975). *Religion in America.* New York: Macmillan Publishing, Co.

Barna, George. (1991). *User Friendly Churches.* Ventura, CA: Ventura Regal Books.

Barnes, Rebecca; Lowry, Lindy. "Special report: The American church in crisis." *Christianity Today.* 21 June 2006.

Berkley, James. (1997). *Leadership handbook of management and administration.* Grand Rapids, MI: Zondervan

Celek, Tim; Zander, Dieter. *Inside the soul of a new generation.* (1996). Grand Rapids, MI: Zondervan

Engelsman, Joy. (2005). "What it takes: Ideas for planning intergenerational worship." *Reformed Worship.*

Frank, Thomas Edward. (2000). *The soul of a congregation.* Nashville, TN: Abingdon Press.

Gibbs, Eddie; Bolger, Ryan K. (2005). *Emerging churches.* Grand Rapids, MI: Baker Academic.

Kinnaman, David; Lyons, Gabe. (2007). *Unchristian: What a new generation really thinks about Christianity... and why it matters.* Ada, MI: Baker Publishing Group.

Ludwig, Glenn E. (2003). *Building an effective youth ministry.* Nashville, TN: Abingdon Press.

McIntosh, Gary L. (2002). *One church four generations.* Grand Rapids, MI. Baker Books.

Rainer, Thom. (2005). *Breakout churches.* Grand Rapids, MI: Zondervan.

Southerland, Dan. (2000). *Transitioning.* Grand Rapids, MI: Zondervan.

Warren, Rick. (1995). *The purpose driven church.* Grand Rapids, MI: Zondervan.

White, James Emery. (2004). *Rethinking the church.* Grand Rapids, MI: Baker House.

Notes

Notes